# BALANCING
Poems of the Female Immigrant Experience
in the Upper Midwest, 1830-1930

## KATHLEEN ERNST

**LITTLE CREEK PRESS**
AND BOOK DESIGN
MINERAL POINT, WISCONSIN

Copyright © 2021 Kathleen Ernst

Little Creek Press®
A Division of Kristin Mitchell Design, Inc.
5341 Sunny Ridge Road
Mineral Point, Wisconsin 53565

Book Design and Project Coordination:
Little Creek Press and Book Design

First Printing
July 2021

All rights reserved

No part of this book may be used or reproduced
in any manner whatsoever without written
permission from the author.

Printed in the United States of America

For more information or to order books,
www.littlecreekpress.com

Library of Congress Control Number: 2021907628

ISBN-13: 978-1-942586-98-2

Front cover photo:
Girl in detention room, Ellis Island, March, 1907
Credit: American Museum of Natural History

Back cover photo:
Portrait of an Italian mother and child just arrived at Ellis Island in 1905,
NMFF.000705 "Peace" (6620099783)

*Oceans, Prairie Bride, Childless, Drowning,* and *Empty* were originally published in *Driftless Review*.

*Lost to the Lake* was originally published in *Halfway to the North Pole: Door County in Poetry*.

*Facing Forward* and *Lost* were included in "Mark My Words" exhibitions at the Pump House Regional Arts Center.

# Table of Contents

PROLOGUE: If Time Is A River .................................. 7

PART 1: **Oceans** .................................................. 9
Trunk ................................................................ 10
Untethered ......................................................... 11
Oceans .............................................................. 12
The Bible ........................................................... 14

PART 2: **Prairies** ................................................ 17
Facing Forward ................................................... 18
Winter Worship ................................................... 19
Breathing ........................................................... 20
Sentinel ............................................................. 21
Prairie Bride ....................................................... 22
Lost ................................................................... 23
Cattle ................................................................. 24
Childless ............................................................ 25
Drowning ............................................................ 26
First Winter ........................................................ 27
Window .............................................................. 28
Softening ............................................................ 30
Empty ................................................................ 32
Restless ............................................................. 33
*Hiraeth* ............................................................. 34

PART 3: **Northwoods and Lakes** ............................ 35
Balancing ........................................................... 38
Stumps .............................................................. 39
Timber Widow ..................................................... 40
In the Root Cellar ................................................ 41

Copper Country............................................42
Rooted....................................................44
Sadie's Rhubarb...........................................45
Lost to the Lake..........................................46
Migration.................................................47

PART 4: **Homesteads**.....................................49
The Applicant.............................................50
Abandoned Claim...........................................51
Threshing.................................................52
Young Schoolteacher.......................................54
Mail-Order Bride..........................................55
Knitting Needles..........................................56
Christmas Orange..........................................58
*Fika*....................................................60
Joy in the Morning........................................62

EPILOGUE: The Oldest Surviving Pioneer....................65

About the Author..........................................67

PROLOGUE
# If Time Is A River

Beware the memories trapped
just below the surface. Touch
the shimmering water with your oar.
See the images ripple and fade.
Watch for the eddies where days
long gone change course,
briefly flowing back, mingling with
newer droplets coursing through,
lingering just long enough
to moisten your fingers.

Wisconsin Historical Society, Image ID 28708.

# PART 1
# Oceans

# Trunk

After the auction, the trunk stood alone like an altar:
constructed by carpenter, bound by blacksmith,
adorned with flowers and scrolls—red-yellow-blue—
by the itinerant painter who'd trudged to their door.
Christina packed bits of Norway into their chest:
butter tub, bridal dress, pewter dipper, flatbread griddle.

At the dock, bellowing cartmen shoved through the throng.
Christina feared the need to keep safe both children and luggage;
had not known she would feel bereft to relinquish the trunk.
No effort was made to respect the lineage of those boxes
piling up shipside; each painted with the owner's name,
and strange words too: *Detroit, Chicago, Milwaukee, St. Paul.*
Christina watched burly strangers row the painted trunks
to the waiting ship and hoist them aboard, gaudy as
a flock of foolish birds offering themselves to winds
bent on blowing them far off-course.

# Untethered

The emigrant women of Dietlingen carried babies and bedrolls
and fat balls of homespun wool as they gathered at the port.
They gave the loose ends of yarn to the weeping
shawl-wrapped women who had come to wave good-bye,
and let the yarn unwind behind as they boarded the ship
soon to buck westward through Atlantic waves.

The emigrant women of Dietlingen pressed to the rail,
looking toward the dock as sailors set flapping, snapping sails.
The ship pranced from the harbor as a purebred filly
might leave her stall, and each woman clutched fibers—
white, gray, brown—twisted well on wheels
in distant valleys and villages, ephemeral tethers
to the mothers and sisters and friends being left behind.

The emigrant women of Dietlingen cupped their hands,
cradling the balls born from bouncing German lambs,
letting salt-damp yarn unwind through trembling fingers.
The wool unspooled too fast, too fast,
until each woman felt her filament slip away.
Soon dozens of strands billowed lightly over the swells,
waving farewell, disappearing like the tail of a fearful mare
galloping back to familiar pastures.

# Oceans

More than the leaving, more than beginning again,
Anna dreaded the voyage. She had read all the letters—
litanies of weevils and rats, smallpox and typhus,
beams creaking doom through furious storms, puking and stink,
regrets and fears, harsh words and tears, foreigners
and friends crammed like cordwood in a coffin-like hold.

All true, and worse, and more.

Still, no one had written of twilight hours at the rail
as the sinking sun streaked the clouds, vermilion and puce.
No one had spoken of night skies that glittered and warmed
like a spangled cloak tucked 'round her shoulders; of strangers
gathered on deck, offering dried plums and zwieback, songs
sung in Flemish or Polish or Greek, somehow understood;

no one had suggested that with no more than a bunk to tend,
she might rest; that the endless debate between wind and water
might whisper of compromise and contentment; that waves
riffling to the horizon might lull her, suspending her between
leaving's grief and arrival's work and worry, poised like a petrel
riding swells between storm peak and valley.

So she mourned again upon arrival: the port's crowded clamor,
barking hucksters and swindlers. Anna and Lars traveled inland
by train and steamship and wagon. They arrived drenched,
the prairie beaten and despondent, all sucking mud and thunder.
She remembered each letter—litanies of loneliness and wildfires,
hail and drought, rattlers coiled beneath beds, wolves' dirges.

All true, and worse, and more.

Still, no one had written of the sweet scent of new-scythed hay.
No one had hinted that Lars's face would glow like sunrise
when their own plow scoured their own soil; that when
it came time to build a barn neighbors would come, speaking
Danish and Swedish and Welsh, some rattling in buckboards,
some trudging miles with hammers and saws and sour cream pies;

no one had suggested that with no more than a cabin to tend,
she might sometimes rest; that when wandering through prairies
the endless whispered conversation between wind and grass spoke
of compromise and contentment; that the blooms riffling to the
horizon might lull her, suspending her between work and worry,
rising like a hawk on warm winds between thunderhead and vale.

# The Bible

How the Oosterbeck men argued over that leather-bound Book!
Fights splintered families, angered friends, fractured
the Dutch Church, parted honest folk as Moses had the Red Sea.
Griet mostly found God in the yeasty scent of bread dough,
her infant daughter's persistent tug at her breast,
the bright satin miracle of tulip fields in bloom.
But when Hendrik sold the farm, the fields, the familiar,
Griet wrapped with care, in a wool blanket, the Bible—
source of conflict, source of comfort too.

From Rotterdam they pitched across the Atlantic to New York City,
traveled further west on a canal boat pulled by plodding mules,
boarded in Buffalo the *Phoenix*, to traverse the Great Lakes.
Griet liked the name, liked to think of her family rising
from the past, from poverty, from arguments about faith.
She prayed as the steamer bucked through storm after storm,
thinking of the Book packed in their chest. She'd sacrificed
to bring it—space that might have held another warm blanket,
spare wooden shoes, a sack of dried peas, an extra shawl.

With four thousand miles behind them, just five miles still to go,
she woke to a new sound, a strange sound, not the steady snap
of pistons, not the propellers' familiar throbbing hum.
Then smoke, screams, pounding footsteps, bellowed curses.
Griet snatched her daughter, clung to Hendrik; they clawed
their way to the deck where in an instant she had to choose
between writhing flames and November's black waves.
She jumped. She jumped and clutched her baby,
sobbed for Hendrik, clung to a crate.

She tried to clench hope as the sky glowed red as Satan.
Hope died as the prayers and pleas faded, one by one;
Griet faded too. So cold. Too cold.
The *Phoenix* sank. For weeks, the drowned drifted ashore.
*So many children*, folks lamented, but men and women too.
The gold in the immigrants' pockets sank, and their trunks,
painted or plain; hoes and axes, chisels and churns.
The lake gave up one prize with the bodies:
the great Bible—source of comfort, source of anguish too.

PART 2
# Prairies

# Facing Forward

In the Old World, Emil muttered prayers over trenchers
of *lutefisk*, peered at the sky and sniffed the air to decide
when to plant potatoes, counted coins before Birgit shopped.
She tended her hearth as she'd been raised to do, an endless
chain of chores, and worn-fingered women doing them.

In the Old World, when the hungry time came,
rye crop blackened with rust, children whimpering,
empty bellies and purses, Emil said *We will go.*
Birgit wept to leave her mother and sisters, *lefse* and cod,
smoke-stained village, mossy gravestones, all she knew.

In the New World, walking west, Birgit bore weight:
an unborn child in front, the toddler on her hip, worry.
When the oxen foundered she knotted her mother's
kale seeds and candlesticks into the shawl tied
over one shoulder; and hefted the rifle too.

But in the New World, Birgit walked with a step lighter
than heels rubbed raw, feet on fire, muscles' ache,
sunburned skin. She walked toward the prairie,
the unexpected promise of possibility, new grace
in her heart, a life not defined before her wedding day,

while Emil trudged behind, dragging an anvil
of doubt and fear, missing his father,
looking over his shoulder; but looking forward, too,
toward the woman he once knew, wondering
what he'd lost, and how she'd come to find it.

# Winter Worship

They arrived in November and found
no preachers in the settlement
of crabbed cabins, towering oaks, prairie.
Time dragged, full of cracked lips, frozen toes,
brittle sunshine, looming shadows.
Logs groaned, ice fractured, men cursed,
children burrowed hollow and dull beneath quilts.
Cora paid her tithes at the woodpile,
perched on a board in the snow,
ax clutched in mittened, frostbit hands.
Chop and haul, chop and haul, bless
the warming muscles, curse the freezing sweat.
Then into the cabin to worship
at the cast-iron altar, source of life yet
insatiable, glowing red as brimstone.

# Breathing

There had been moments—on the stinking ship,
in the shrieking ports, on the smoke-belching train—
when she couldn't suck in air enough to satisfy her lungs;
when she fought for stillness—fisting her skirt,
clenching her teeth, willing her pounding heart to slow;
while her man mumbled to his friends, oblivious.

Now there were moments—in the dewy-dawn garden,
on the fragrant prairie path, in the open wagon—
when the air was rich and sweet and cool in her lungs,
when she couldn't be still—picking sunflowers,
marveling at meadowlarks, twirling 'til her heart pounded;
while her man mumbled to his mule, oblivious.

# Sentinel

Their journey ended where an ancient oak stood sentinel
on the prairie—umbrella of branches embracing
a pocket of sky, bell of roots anchored deep in the sod.
Nannie loved the oak and Sam loved her, so as those first
months passed his plow sliced soil well beyond its shade,
and his ax stayed slung on the wall. She crept daily to her
private bower between dark cabin and endless sky.

She carried relics there too: the bleached bison skull found
over the rise, the notched arrowhead spotted amongst
creekside pebbles, a perfect china cup of cobalt and cream
inexplicably placed beside the ruts of long-gone,
iron-rimmed wheels. She drowsed, and dreamed
of lumbering beasts, and brown-skinned men,
and women weeping for things lost or left behind.

Nannie watched from beneath the green canopy as Sam
wrenched bluestem and side-oats gramma from the earth,
roots longer than she was tall. One morning she unfastened
the clasp of her only pretty, a locket he'd gifted her, now cradling
a wispy curl from the infant girl they'd buried weeks back
along the trail. And she left it there, by the skull and the sharp
stone and the china cup, hoping that one day someone might
dream of her, while the ancient oak stood sentinel.

# Prairie Bride

How Lutie hated that goose!
A stringy gander, ruling his dusty domain
with hisses and snaps, neck weaving snake-like,
tracking Lutie's progress across the yard; his
grating honks when wild cousins crossed the clouds,
frustrated flaps of clipped wings, raising puffs of dust
among the gray-white slimes left to soil Lutie's hem.

Oh, Lutie hated that goose.
But still, when the smokehouse sat empty,
cellar shelves bare, and Lutie's man—
a distant plowing speck against the sky—
craved meat; when Lutie felt weak against her heavy hoe,
full buckets, kicking bulge beneath her skirt—
still, she couldn't grasp the ax.

Lutie wasn't afraid of grabbing that goose,
all crashing wings and glittering eyes;
nor of the heavy heft of oak and steel,
the swing and the blood, the plucking and guts.
But her marrow froze when she thought
of incessant wind blowing through a yard
abruptly gone still, and silent.

# Lost

From the train, the prairie looked flat as a cracker.
Lena didn't learn until settling on their new place
that the land rose and fell like a restless sea;
that the tall grasses hid swales that swallowed
the silk bonnet blown from her head
while they wagoned to town, the plump ruffed grouse
she'd hoped to shoot for Sunday dinner, and—
as she pegged out wet laundry, humming a hymn—
the child who toddled from her side.

# Cattle

Much was wondrous strange in the new world:
primordial cranes chortling in the marshland,
ancient chipped-stone tools thrust aside by the plow,
pumpkins grown larger than arms could embrace,
grubbed oak and elm trees left to smolder like waste—
and Yankee men milking their cows.

Solveig came from a steep place where strong-handed women
tended cattle: squatting on the stools, cheeks pressed
against warm flanks, seeking comfort on sleet-freeze nights
in the cattle shed; climbing each spring to the high farm,
all wildflowers and golden light, ancient alchemy tingling unseen
in their palms as they transformed milk to butter, porridge, cheese.

In this flat place Yankee ladies smirked behind lace handkerchiefs,
shunned their own barns, spoke of foreign-born women
"yoked to the herd." Solveig pitied them for what they didn't know
about the beasts grazing on lush grass, about the strength
of a greedy calf sucking drops of milk from fingers, about
the reassuring *zing zing zing* as warm milk filled the pail;
feminine wisdom, ancient power.

# Childless

William loathed wild indigo, lush green pillows on the prairie,
poison to his cattle. He tried to wrench it from the earth,
cursing roots clenched by six feet of stubborn soil. He ignored
the pallid flower spikes which drooped, as Laura sometimes did,
in this place of endless wind and sky. She studied the plants,
so well-footed, surviving gale and neglect.

In damp spring, once the last snow melted into the soil, she sank
daily by the small shrubs, fingering verdant stems
and blossoms pale as new butter. Solitary bees fumbled
about the blooms, preparing for their sons and daughters;
founder queens that crawled from underground nests
much as Laura crept blinking from the cabin.

In summer heat, duskywings fluttered among the indigo—
moth-like creatures, sucking sweet nectar, wise but drab,
a mottled brown. No one admired them but Laura.
She searched for the butterflies' tiny pearl-eggs on the leaves;
watched as caterpillars emerged to gorge, safe,
on the greens too toxic for cows to graze.

By autumn Laura loved wild indigo: deep-anchored,
repellant to the clumsy, haven for the fragile.
But she turned away when sharp winds
sent fat shiny pods tumbling over the prairie,
scattering seeds beyond the horizon.

# Drowning

Helene remembered when her tall man had a taller dream:
ripe-tawny rye rippling ocean-like beneath the breeze.
She'd had dreams too: gleaming jars of currant jelly,
air dank and musty from overflowing onion bins.
Whitewashed church, linen altar cloths to wash and press,
Sunday picnics spread on planks. A school bell's distant peal.
Lamplit evenings spent stringing apple rings to dry,
reading letters from home, watching her towheads
scratch sums and hearing spelling lists recited.
Her husband bursting home and happy from the mill,
with empty wagon and full pockets, offering
a sea-green ribbon he'd bought for her hair.

# First Winter

When the log walls groaned with cold
and wind stabbed through the cracks,
she had nothing to do inside
but scrape frost from the window,
watch the larder empty, inexorable;
hunch by the fireplace, listening
to wolves howl in the night.

When the air was brittle and still,
and marrow froze in the bones,
she had nothing to do outside
but flounder through drifts to the stable,
watch the grain bin empty, inexorable;
hunt through the piney woods, hearing
wolves pad behind, just out of reach.

No books to read, no wool to spin,
no harness to mend, no yarn to knit,
no children to teach, no cotton to sew,
just ice-dark nights and glitter-bright days
and nothing to do
but wait.

# Window

They had only one, cradled home in the buckboard
swaddled in quilts. He set it square; she washed it
every day with water hauled from the creek, and zeal.
She watched the world beyond the bubbled pane:
green spears of new growth; purple coneflowers;
the bronze-gold of ripening wheat.

Winter's first blizzard: she swaddled him in scarves,
and watched him stagger past the glass, bound for the stable,
last milking in late day's blue-white blur. Frost formed
on the pane as she waited, tracing his steps in her mind.
Snow gathered on the sill; wind slapped the glass.
She scraped a peep hole clear with a knife. Her heart

slowly froze with the waiting, first rimed with frost, then iced
to its core. Light faded, the snow now deep as the sill.
All night she howled with the wind, with the wondering: was
he safe with the cow, inhaling her scent, borrowing her warmth,
sipping her milk? Had he missed the barn, stumbled blind
onto the prairie, died ice-pelted and calling *her* name?

Dawn found her dry-eyed, needing fuel, imprisoned by a drift heaved against the door. She touched the precious pane, fragile glaze, last defense against the wind, and freezing; a brittle skin she could shatter. She might crawl through and find him, her warmth and comfort. Or she might find only triumphant wind, frigid and cruel, her own certain end.

With trembling fingers, she grasped the sadiron—irrelevant now— and heaved.

# Softening

Beth and Daniel were raised with right angles: New England's town squares, pragmatism, rows of beans and okra seeds plumbed with string; sober churches, picket fences, frugality, cedar shakes row upon row. Two centuries ago, their ancestors unpacked on American soil, stoic and stern, good Yankee stock.

When they moved west, Beth packed with care: butcher knives, butter churns, practicality; woolen socks, casks of cornmeal and flour, common sense; quilts with bindings mitered sharp and square. No room in the oaken chests for Mother's vase, sentiment, best Sunday bonnet stitched of black silk.

They made their new home on the prairie, a rippling river of grass, swells and swales. Daniel unpacked methodically: gleaming ax, leather gloves, scouring plow; seed corn, firm goals, portable forge. Beth unpacked too, brisk and determined: chopping block, egg beater, resolve; lye soap, lanterns, neat-labeled packets of seeds.

But lupines bloomed past the garden plot plumbed with string. Sandhill cranes chortled primeval; upland sandpipers whistled among pinwheels of prairie phlox, violet and pink. As summer unspooled Beth sometimes left off her scrubbing, her mending, her stewing. Hanging out sheets, the sun and scent gave her pause.

Then a rain-damp dawn revealed liatris and butterfly milkweed blurring toward the horizon. The meadowlarks called her name. After Daniel left to break and scour, Beth let herself be beckoned, to embrace whorls of wild roses, tumbling clouds, shimmering dragonflies, a world gone ripe and round.

# Empty

The immigrant trunk, where she'd tried to tuck
    the essence of home—an embroidered collar,
    her mother's prayer book—among the fry pans
    and hatchels and sturdy boots.

The cradle, after her daughter died.
    Faded blue blanket gone for a shroud,
    no lingering scent of urine or milk,
    no echo of chortles or cries.

His seat at the table, more and more often
    as the wheat was devoured by chinch bugs,
    so thick on the ground that her boots crunched
    as she walked the scoured field.

The jug as well, cast aside on the threshing floor
    meant for sprawling piles of golden grain on canvas,
    the measured tread of oxen or the rhythmic beat of flails,
    baskets brimming with winnowed wheat.

And the cracked blue crock on the pantry shelf
    Where she tucked coins earned
    selling her noodled geese on market day.
    Empty now, set a bit off-angle, perhaps ashamed.

# Restless

It was hard on a marriage, when one wanted to sink deep roots;
the other, to roll on west like a wagon wheel.
Marie learned not to grow close to the neighbor-women,
not to plant fruit trees, not to love the land.
She learned to say, *Looks like we'll be moving on* calmly,
over the quilting frame at the local bee;
to smile politely at condolences.
She learned to pack their trunks efficiently,
taking what they must, leaving the rest;
and to pack a wagon, too, with the oxen in mind.
She learned to live with the disappointment in Luke's eyes.
*We could stay,* he'd plead.
But she never learned how to turn away
from the western horizon; how to break its spell,
how to ignore its promises.

# *Hiraeth*

The old Welsh women knew what it meant
to yearn for a home left behind, unattainable.
When they sat spinning, their minds conjured
childhood days spent playing on the floor
as their mothers' wheels rattled, endlessly familiar.
When they pinched up flour, salt, tangy yeast,
they mourned the certainty that their own
*bara brith* would never taste like Granny's.
When they greeted friends in the puddled churchyard
grief misted their eyes, rasped in their throats.
When they swept the front porch they sometimes paused,
gripping the broom, blindly staring east, homesick
for a shrouded land they scarce recalled.

PART 3

# Northwoods and Lakes

# Balancing

They traveled weary-far from Hungary to
the homestead—wagon, steam ship, railroad, shoes.
The last eighteen miles wound through cutover land,
rain sheeting down, chill wind knifing across
the ravaged land; the lanes loggers had cleared
for their straining horses now a sucking mucky mire.
Kornelia and her family stepped stump to stump,
her holding an infant, and by the hand
a four-year-old, once excited, now fretful.

How strange that her life had come to this:
Balancing—
from stump to stump, from Old World to New,
from dreaming bride to resolute wife,
one foot rooted solid, the other suspended in air.

# Stumps

Long after Yankees and Germans and Swedes
had broken prairie sod, farm dreams
brought Esko and Asta from Finland.
*Go north*, said the land agent at the Milwaukee dock.
*Great land, great price.* Asta watched as Esko
signed papers, tucked them away, eyes wide with wonder.

*A crop is already waiting!* called the agent, and smiled.
Esko smiled too, not knowing it was acres of stumps
needing harvest, left behind by the timbermen.

Asta couldn't bear to watch *sisu*-hearted
Finnish men battle to clear their land,
neighbors helping neighbors, groaning and swearing.
Dynamite took three of Esko's fingers.
A spooked mare crushed Koskinen's leg.
Jokela died when a snapping cable cracked his skull.

All that first spring Asta fought the root-laced soil
with a grub hoe, planting turnips and rutabagas
among the stumps, training sickly pumpkin vines
to trail among them. The earth was sand, the topsoil thin;
the growing season much too short.

By first frost their money was gone. Esko was too,
walking west toward the lumber camp where he would
spend six months cutting timber, hauling timber,
leaving acres and miles of stumps
for other wives' men to fight.

# Timber Widow

Each fall, when the corn was cut, turnips dug, firewood stacked,
Mikko packed his bear-hide mittens, scratchy wool shirts,
long johns ordered from the Sears catalog, and trudged north.
He'd work in the camp all winter, a piney world of deep snow,
smoky bunkhouse, drying wool socks draped over rafters,
crosscut saws and skidders, oxen snorting white puffs of steam.
He left Tuovi with a silence the boys' clamor never filled;
empty bed, freezing dawns; shuffling through hip-high drifts
to milk the cows and feed the chickens, facing blizzards and bears,
fingering coins kept in an old lard can; short days and long nights,
sometimes letters, sometimes not.

Mikko tramped home in spring mud, muscled, roughened by coarse
company and heavy food, bringing whittled gifts for his family,
horses and birds and a heart-shaped spoon. They reacquainted
themselves amidst planting, freshened cows, roofs to repair and
berries to can; long days, short nights, a bed grown crowded,
remembered pleasures, snores that silenced the ticking clock; each
of her choices re-examined, sometimes changed, sometimes not.

Years passed bisected by coming and going, winter and summer,
alone and together; Tuovi's hands ever reluctant to seize the reins;
reluctant to release them too. It took six months to adjust
to his leaving, six more to accept his coming home.

# In the Root Cellar

Jonas thought poor planning spurred Ruth's trips, for
she trudged daily through snow, sleet stinging her cheeks,
insidious slush creeping through her shoe seams,
numb fingers clawing at the wooden latch. Inside, only
the wind stopped. Damp air seeped cold into her bones,
filled her lungs with old turnips' heavy mustiness.
The scraped-smooth earthen floor clutched a dormant chill.
Centipedes skittered behind crates of sand-packed carrots,
sauerkraut barrels, heaps of Hubbard squash.

Ruth filled her basket quickly: one rutabaga, two beets.
Then she slid her fingers over cool glass jars, dim in the gloom
but recalled in fruited glory, purple, crimson, plum.
They conjured love-tumble nights and child-laughter days,
hay-scented sun and sticky-sweat skin, brimming harvest and
visiting friends, travel and abundance, tastes tart or tangy-sweet:
spiced apple butter, puckering rhubarb, honeyed blackberries,
frost-kissed grapes, currants simmered with maple syrup.

These jars she counted daily, eking them out, making them last.
She'd sealed sunshine beneath their zinc lids, plump with promise,
holding her hand, leading her toward a distant spring.

# Copper Country

*I thought the damn bell would never ring*, Drago declared
when he and nine other men drooped to the boardinghouse
from the mine—trammers all, who pushed overloaded ore cars,
eight thousand feet below sunshine. Bosses respected
the Croatian men's monstrous strength, suspected their politics,
made it difficult for them to get ahead. Purchased horses
were better tended; laboring men too easily replaced
by the next hollow-eyed immigrants new from the boat.

Branka knew all about the shifts, the deafening mechanical roar,
the red dust coating their skin and their lungs. Her own man
had not lived long enough to die of disease, crushed instead
by falling rock; their farm dreams died too, leaving Branka only
debts and two young daughters. So she built bunks, posted a sign;
cooked cauldrons of fish stew, baked mounds of *lepinja* bread;
scrubbed shirts stiff with sweat that stunk of blasting powder,
raised rutabagas, nursed the baby's smallpox.

*Damn ten-hour shifts*, Mislav grumbled now as the men settled
at the table, grabbing platters with scabbed and scarred hands,
ravenous for pickled beets and pickled fish Branka bartered
for a promise of mending. She ground coffee, chopped wood,
and hauled water, knowing that by the time she'd scoured
the last plate the miners would be arguing, joking, playing poker;
keeping her girls awake in the attic. She would sing them to sleep
and darn their stockings; squint weary at her accounts in a
kerosene lantern's yellow light while snores rumbled the rafters.

She grieved for her man; grieved too for her homesick boarders—
although not one ever considered just how mightily
she might yearn for a mere ten-hour shift, and a quitting bell.

# Rooted

Before leaving Poland, hopeless and landless and hungry,
Aleksandra stole seeds, stitched them precious as gems
into her hem. All that first year she had little to serve
Janusz after a day in the mines—soup of milk and
potatoes, dark bread kneaded up from the middlings
left behind after flour was sacked at the mill. Sometimes
she leaned close to the fire as sleet lashed the shingles,
the seeds poured into tiny piles on a scrap of muslin
so she could study, finger, measure, dream.

Cabbage and carrots, beets and beans, leeks and lettuce—
minuscule promises of better days, food pickled or crunched fresh,
full bellies and fleshed-out cheeks; tiny tokens, too, of the
mother she'd left behind. As much as Janusz longed for all
that was new, Aleksandra yearned to prepare food
as her grandmothers had; to root herself here with
the tastes that lingered from long-cold fires,
smoke-black hearthstones, broken dishes, and love.

# Sadie's Rhubarb

No ephemeral fronds!
Sadie's pie plants punched fist-like through the earth each spring,
fierce and explosive, sprays of sturdy stalks, platter-sized leaves.

No gentle hues!
Sadie's pie plants boasted stems of ruby red, deep burgundy;
ruffled leaves a rich green envied by lesser plants.

Nothing sweet and polite!
Sadie's pie plants were all pucker and strings, sassy and sour;
daring passing children, challenging the cook.

Sadie loved those pie plants: first freshening of spring,
loyal through summer heat; diced and stewed
into pies and pastries, gravy and bread—true bounty.

# Lost to the Lake

The keeper walks at night, they say,
with lantern held high, searching for his children.
Perhaps he'd been the one to study the pearly dawn,
and nod: *You may go.* Perhaps he'd held the boat
as they clambered aboard, and shoved them out
to the waves, and watched as the oldest set the oars.

The children were rowing to school, they say,
ten miles across the passage from St. Marten's Island.
Perhaps they'd gone too far to turn back when a squall
frenzied the waves. Perhaps they were almost
to Washington Island when the boat swamped, plunging
them into Lake Michigan's churning depths.

Perhaps a lunch pail washed ashore, a basket packed
with gingersnaps, a baseball, a bonnet, a slate. No trace
of the children was ever found on stony beach,
in fisherman's net, or gently bobbing in secluded cove.
The keeper walks at night, they say, searching for his children;
but no one dares mention their mother.

# Migration

Each spring the lighthouse women watched
island-hopping migrants come, and go:
clouds of monarch butterflies flittering on the lilac hedge,
furtive yellow-patched warblers flirting in the apple trees,
flocks of squawking jays stalking brassy and shrill on the lawn,
jewel-winged dragonflies dancing in the lake-born breeze,
boiling balls of rough-winged hawks rising on warm columns of air
before—like the others—soaring north.

Each spring the lighthouse women wondered—
Where had they come from? Where would they go?—and
pondered geography, scouring the books (chosen by others)
in the library box, brought by the tender each month
and lugged up the steps from the dock. These women conjured
images of verdant jungles, steaming and damp, tried to imagine
frosted tundra, wind-whipped and chill, all the while
planting onions, pumping washwater, pegging out laundry, and
picking delicate blue forget-me-nots to place in a vase on the sill.

PART 4

# Homesteads

# The Applicant

At fourteen, Kari climbed alone to the mountain *seter*
after her mother died. She spent the summer milking cows,
wrestling goats, churning butter, making cheese: soft *gjetost*,
cooked *kokeost, brunost* sweet and salty. She soured cream
for porridge. and scoured tubs, humming as the sun flamed low.

At seventeen, Kari married a fisherman, farmed
alone the rocky rented plot, and miscarried a child
that had yet to quicken. She grieved but spent the spring
planting barley and potatoes, the summer weeding beans,
the fall drying herbs, cutting hay, pickling cabbage.

At nineteen, Kari listened trembling to a storm shriek down
the coast, lashing the northern seas; paced alone by
the empty boatshed. She spent the frigid winter listening
to mice scamper, making *lefse*, ever waiting and watching
for a man who never came home. The landlord said she must go.

At twenty-one, Kari walked travel-worn to the land agent's office.
The dough-faced clerk fretted, spoke of loneliness and labor,
broken dreams and forfeit land, not knowing that she spoke
no English but knew the language of work; that she knew how to
befriend cows and buntings; that she'd come too far to fail now.

# Abandoned Claim

The berries grew best on the broken land,
hacked bare with grub hoes
by a man and woman who'd finally
lost heart, given up, moved back east.
Lottie prowled brambled furrows, ravenous;
fingers eager for juicy-sweet raspberries,
blackberries, gobbled and gulped in fistfuls.
After frigid months of peas, beans, prunes
and dried apples she was ravenous, craving
morsels ripe and luscious. Still,
as Lottie filled mouth, buckets, basins,
she almost glimpsed the neighbors broken by this land,
watching as she feasted guilty on their failure.

# Threshing

Through the window Gerde can see the men.
The long belt flaps and slaps taut between
hissing steam engine and rattling threshing machine.
Her man points, hollers, gestures with boots planted wide.
He sets some to raking, some to pitching bundles of wheat
from ever-waiting, piled-high wagons. Clean grain
pours from the chute into sacks; clouds of winnowed chaff
billow into a blazing sky. Bits cling fuzzy to the farmers'
sweaty skin, useless to even the most frugal.
By suppertime only the strongest still work with easy grace;
the rest—panting, gulping switchel from flasks—
have winnowed themselves to the ancient oak's shade.

In Gerde's kitchen the iron cookstove, rubbed to a gleam
with newsprint, squats beneath bubbling ironware pots
and heavy skillets. Neighbor women stride through the open door,
swatting flies, bearing pies and doughnuts. Gerde clenches
a scarred wooden spoon, pointing, gesturing, sometimes stirring,
feet planted firm on the brick floor. She sets some to slicing
rye bread, others to counting plates; lets the giggling girls
carry hampers of sandwiches and boiled eggs to the field
at mid-morning. When the steamy air is thick with coffee and
*sauerbraten's* tang Gerde inspects offerings spread
on the linen-covered plank table in the back yard. Some bowls
and plates she positions within easy reach of the ravenous men

who will soon stalk back to eat. But some—overcooked potatoes
brought by the new bride, a cherry pie from the slattern who can't
roll a crust lighter than lead, scorched *kuchens* and bitter beer—
Gerde winnows to a side table.

When the wheat field is stubbled and the kitchen grazed bare
the threshing rig steams on to the next farm. These brief hazy days
lay bare rutted earth and garter snakes long hidden by the grain;
lay bare, too, human chaff winnowed from the heavy tray of pride
and expectation. Gerde smiles, knowing her man measured up
nicely; knowing too, by platters scraped clean, that she did as well.

# Young Schoolteacher

The hardest part wasn't teaching boys one year younger
and six inches taller than her; all brawn and pranks,
crammed elbows, bent knees behind too-small desks;

not the little ones either, hesitant whispers,
homesick whimpers, all wet britches and spilled inkpots,
hunched shoulders, feet dangling above the floor.

It wasn't the need to arrive at dawn, tramping through drifts,
stinging cheeks, numb fingers; fires to light in the frigid school,
dumping ashes, washing windows, dusting desks;

not the hash of teaching eight grades at once, sums and stories
and endless recitations, earnest or faltering; not the boarding out
with strangers, cot in a corner, two weeks here, two weeks there;

nor the press of planning the Christmas pageant, coaching
the mumbling, prompting the stumbling; skits and poems
and carols, costumes to stitch from donated scraps, simple

gifts to make for the parents who would leave their chores
on a bitter night to squeeze into student desks, proud and
watchful, while local bachelors crammed in at the back.

Hardest was the incessant need to glance past frosted panes,
assessing the sky, wary of change; stepping outside to sniff the air
while the students ate lunches kept warm in tin pails by the stove,

watching the first flakes sift from clouds that might hold flurries
or raging blizzard; the safety of twenty children—five to fifteen,
some miles from their homes—worn on her shoulders like iron.

# Mail-Order Bride

In Switzerland, on the first day of spring, the villagers rose
before dawn. By the time a buttery sun spilled over jagged peaks
the procession had formed: cows brushed, belled, and garlanded
with primrose and gentians, knowing goats eager for fresh greens,
milling flocks of new-shorn sheep.

Young men climbed with casks, blankets, and axes lashed
on backboards; young women with baskets of bread and candles,
straining cloths and rennet. First-time boys capered with pride.
Accompanied by the clappers' metallic clang, the travelers sang
the ancient song: *On the alps above waits a glorious life.*

Lara left the trail with her cows at a lower meadow; the shepherds
and their sheep climbed higher; the frisking goats and their tenders
higher still. Summer promised roses, grass, and edelweiss,
the sparkle and splash of iced mountain springs, churning and
cheese-making in the high chalets, alpenhorns heralding vespers....

Now Lara woke in a pancake place of unbroken sky, with nowhere
to lift her gaze; no promise of sweet high summer. She wept
when the prairie wind finally warmed and warned of spring,
this cheesemaker's daughter, now come to a land where snowmelt
meant just a sloppy-mud slog to the barn.

# Knitting Needles

Karin could not bear another child—not with
nine already, the youngest five, and herself
finally free of diapers and drool; not with three
more buried up on the hill, each coffined

with a piece of her heart; not with her weary womb.
There are ways, her wise-woman neighbor said—
Inger, who stopped after twelve babies, each
a sunrise joy, each a midnight thief too.

One morning after the young ones gamboled
toward school like spring lambs, after the older boys
trudged willing to the fields with their unknowing father,
Karin took her knitting—creamy yarn nested in

a woven willow basket—to the bedroom. She sat
on the bed, on the tumbling blocks quilt stitched from
blue-yellow-green scraps of her children's clothes.
She hefted the needles, fingered the blunt blades.

Kristian had carved them from Danish cedar so she'd always
hold home in her hands. She'd knit on the ship, baby booties
and ribbed sweaters, loops upon loops, Merino wool scouring
the wood smooth, as all her knowing unskeined behind.

New World, new home, they had lived in her pocket. One tip
had turned guts at butchering time, reeking and raw,
for sausage casings; one had flipped Christmas *aebleskivers*,
pale sweet puffs of solace in the cast iron pan.

One tip had poked holes in her garden's dark loam,
ripe for the seed tucked safe in the earth, nursed
by rain, birthed by springtime sun; cabbage and beans
but dahlias too, like those she had grown in Denmark.

Now a wren trilled beyond the window. The dahlias
leaned toward the sun. Karin stroked the needles and
wished she knew which choice would bind her family,
and which would cause its unraveling.

# Christmas Orange

He snatched it from the crate at the general store;
wrapped it in his woolen muffler, tucked it tenderly
into an inside pocket. On the long, frigid drive,
sleigh runners *whushing* through icy ruts, he smiled
through his shivers, seeing her pierce the rind with a fingernail,

peeling it with a thumb, separating sections gently.
He thought she might close her eyes as she savored it,
summer-sweet juice on her tongue, such a change
from rutabagas and rye rolls and salt pork.
And she did relish it.

The gift became a promise, an orb of spring, talisman against
blizzards and blows and bleak gray skies. She liked to stare
at the ball of color on its barren shelf in the whitewashed room.
*Peel it*, he said, but she shook her head. Even a hungry man
might not devour his last bite of food.

The gift became geography, a globe, a reminder
of what lay beyond the horizon. She liked to finger the peel,
where tiny tracks meandered like river valleys in a foreign land.
*Taste it*, he said, but she shook her head. Even those rooted,
as she was, might not destroy their map.

The gift became a magic carpet, lush and exotic, transport
to adventure. She liked to press it to her nose, sucking in
the faint musky scent to mask stale sweat and rotting potatoes.
*Eat it*, he said, but she shook her head. Even a child
who dreams of sailing does not break the bottle that holds the ship.

KATHLEEN ERNST

The gift became a teller of tales, born as it was on a tree wet with
tropical rain. She liked to imagine dark-skinned pickers, voices
raised in indecipherable songs, flitting birds feathered bright.
*Now!* he said, but she still shook her head. Like Scheherazade,
she dared not stop the stories.

When new shoots poked through mud outside the cabin,
the orange turned its own springtime hue, fusty gray-green.
*You wasted it*, he said, but she shook her head.
She closed her eyes, as he'd once imagined, and spoke softly:
*It has fed me for months, and I savor it still.*

# *Fika*

Decades ago, Linnea filled her tin box with Swedish rye
and crammed it into the trunk. Andreas brought
his own seed. His for the ground, hers for the pot.

In Wisconsin she roasted her grain in the skillet over
a campfire with an umbrella in one hand, and ground it
as best she could; a poor substitute for coffee.

When that ran out she wrenched three-foot chicory roots
from the soil to scrub, slice, dry, roast, grind; made coffee
on her tiny stove; brewed thick, black, and bitter.

The next year, Andreas brought molasses home from
the store. Linnea added a dollop as she parched cornmeal,
and brewed that; he smiled at the hint of sweetness.

Only at Christmas did her children smell the sharp scent
of beans in the skillet, hear their crunch in the grinder,
know the dark roasted taste of true coffee.

Crops grew, trees fell, sows gave birth to piglets.
Andreas added a lean-to, cattle barn, root cellar;
swore allegiance to the flag, cast ballots at the town hall.

Linnea found time to piece quilts and grow hollyhocks
but did not know success until she was able to brew a pot
of fresh coffee every day; to welcome the preacher

with a steaming mug, to warm Andreas on bitter nights,
to usher unexpected friends inside where a table was set
with pretty china cups and plates of cardamom-scented buns.

*We have done well*, Linnea sometimes told Andreas
as she poured, and while he spoke proud of crops and stock
she'd smile and sip her coffee, at last content.

# Joy in the Morning

She'd been raised to rise brisk from bed.
*The devil hates a hurry*, Mama used to say,
*so meet the day headlong.*

Here, on her own claim, she rose in the dark,
lit the oil lamp, made egg coffee in the enamel pot,
lifted it with a scrap of turkey-red calico,
then took a steaming mug to the front step
to watch the sun yawn over the horizon,
yellow as an egg yolk. That pearly time
between night and day was so still
she heard bees buzzing in the clover,
a meadowlark whistling from a milkweed stalk,
her own Orpingtons clucking behind the shed door.
The sun burnished nodding wheat heads like gold,
and the cat rubbed against her ankles, and the coffee
was strong and hot; the day, beguiling.

Photo: Author's collection.

EPILOGUE

# The Oldest Surviving Pioneer

*Was it worth it?* asked the restless reporter, bored;
and when the old woman didn't answer, he said again:
*Was it worth it? Leaving all you knew, your home,
to begin a new life in America?*

And still she didn't answer. She didn't like
this impatient young man, tapping his pencil,
exhaling his sighs; didn't like his foolish questions,

as if there weren't butterflies and bones
on both sides of the Atlantic; as if lives lived
could be sorted like fresh eggs from bad,
kept like sweet cream or tossed like sour milk,
wrapped around sharp shoulders like Cotswold wool
or set aside like scratchy new linen,
inhaled like sweet pine smoke or waved away
like the stink of tainted meat in the air; as if
both Old World and New weren't
equally platted with gardens and graves

# About the Author

Kathleen Ernst is an award-winning author, educator, and social historian whose interest in the immigrant experience began while working at Old World Wisconsin, an outdoor ethnic museum in Eagle. She is the author of forty books, including the Chloe Ellefson Mysteries, *A Settler's Year: Pioneer Life Through the Seasons*, and historical fiction for young readers. Honors for Kathleen's work include the American Heritage Women in the Arts Recognition Award for Literature from the National Society of the Daughters of the American Revolution, a Major Achievement Award from the Council For Wisconsin Writers, the Sterling North Legacy Award for Children's Literature, and an Emmy Award for Children's Instructional Programming. Visit **www.kathleenernst.com** for more information.

CPSIA information can be obtained
at www.ICGtesting.com
Printed in the USA
LVHW010444020222
709936LV00011B/1551